Claim Your
Identity

If You Know Who You Are,
You Will Know What To Do!

Stan E. DeKoven

Claim Your Identity

If You Know Who You Are, You Will Know What To Do

Stan E. DeKoven

Copyright ©2017 by Stan DeKoven

ISBN 978-1-61529-190-8

Vision Publishing
P.O. Box 1680
Ramona, CA 92065
1-800-9-VISION
www.booksbyvision.org

Table of Contents

Author's Introduction

I suppose I have thought about this topic since I was about eight years old. Prior to eight, like most boys and girls, I enjoyed the blissful status of being the center of the universe, shared by few (siblings mainly; few friends), under the tutelage of my practically perfect parents who loved me unconditionally (a blissful delusion, of course). As a young boy, I lived with a few assumptions…God is…mom and dad will always be there…food, clothing, and shelter, never in abundance, but always available, would be magically provided, and the New York Yankees would win The World Series (remember, this was the early 60's). Well, life was not always bliss, but I assumed it was good. I had little self-consciousness, did not worry about self-esteem, was not that self-aware or self-assured…just a kid with some assumptions…based upon little else than simple trust. By and large, most of us start out that way.

Certainly, some people are more self-aware than others (mainly girls) but our basic trust in the goodness of life, mom, dad, teacher, pastors, politicians (ok, maybe I am pushing it some) is a part of our universal narrative. Somewhere along the line, most of these naïve understandings change…we grow up! Even before the nightmare and wonder of puberty, our trust, institutional and personal is at least challenged, leading to greater awareness of our vulnerabilities, less confidence in our earlier assumptions, leading us further to reevaluate every aspect of our lives…unconditional love, faith, hope, even life itself. Wow, thankfully we don't face all of this at once. How overwhelming that would be. Perhaps not necessarily in dramatic style, but face it we will.

This facing of ourselves, our inner self, is essential to growing up. As Socrates aptly stated, "The unexamined life, (which is somewhat inevitable and unavoidable), is not worth living." This examination, often done in light of new knowledge, education and experience, peer review, unfortunate circumstances, can be difficult at best for those of us raised in less than perfect (whatever that is) environments. Yet face and evaluate we must, as we slowly, sometimes painfully learn more about who we are in relation to others, and then as believers, in light of God's revelation of himself in the Word of God, living (Jesus) and written. In time, we become acutely aware that, rather than being the blissful center of the universe, we are flawed, perhaps broken, definitely sinners. Thus, worth less than we previously dreamed. If we are a "good" believer (I came to faith at 12; a good age I think), we might be less wounded than others. But since our core identity, whether we are liked or not, believe we are good or bad, worth more or less is established by around age 8. Consequently, though I had a wonderful and relatively young beginning with Christ, I never felt "good" or "acceptable" ...but I tried really, really, really hard to please mom, dad, teacher, Pastor, God, Santa (hedging my bets) but to limited avail...as I always failed to measure up..." Never going to make it" and "not good enough" were refrains often ringing in my head. I heard all the words about God's love, his grace, mercy, kindness...but I couldn't relate, as I also continuously heard, directly or indirectly, that I could never be what God expected...Holy, Holy, Holy!!! But, I didn't give up. I embraced the false belief that I was a sinner saved by grace...eternally! I would never be what God wanted since I was so overwhelmingly damaged by sin, willful and inherited, but at least I was going to Heaven…Hallelujah! Ugh!

Well, I must say I believed this for a long time; but not anymore. You see, my childhood perception, though naive and immature, is closer to the truth. Not that I am the center of the universe, but I am the apple of God's eye. As a child of God, I have worth, not based upon what I do (I want to do well, but not because I have to in order to please) but simply who I am…God's child; his son, his heir, his creation and joy.

God so loved me he sent the perfect role model for me to follow (Jesus) and provides the greatest wisdom to guide me (Holy Spirit and Word of God). I am who God says I am…but the key is believing it, and that is what this little book, inspired by life, preached in Fontana, with input from both Dr. Barry and Dr. Ken Chant, is all about. You see, finding one's true identity is not hard…that's why for so many it is unbelievable.

Dr. Stan

*"I'm strong to the finish,
'cause I eats me Spinach,
I'm Popeye the sailor man!"*

Chapter One:
Two Important Things

There are two things a proper concept of identity can do for a person. But first, let's provide some definition.

EM Griffin defines identity as, "the mind's-eye picture we have of ourselves." This can be positive or negative. As he stated, "we may not like what we see, but at least we know what is there." This definition assures us of the importance of having a well-focused, and proper concept of our identity. This proper concept is important for many reasons. Firstly, it shows us how special and unique we are. We derive comfort from knowing that we have been uniquely created by God and that he knows us individually; there is no one else who is exactly like us. Knowing that we are special and uniquely made by God also makes us conscious of the fact that he has a special plan and purpose for our lives and nothing and no one can thwart that plan, perhaps excepting ourselves. Having a clarity of identity and our uniqueness eliminates much of the stress that comes from comparison, competition, and striving when relating to others.

The second reason a well-focused, proper concept of identity is important is that it allows us to know what we can expect from ourselves. When we know what to expect from ourselves we can move forward in life with more confidence and less worry. This is true for seemingly "bad" people as well. They have a realistic image of who they are and they move forward boldly and usually accomplish their goals. Additionally, once we know what to expect from ourselves we can concentrate on other people's actions and external circumstances. This is especially true for Christians. If our identity is ultimately rooted and grounded in Christ, it will remain stable and our divine purpose will be fulfilled (more on this to follow).

Identity vs Self-Esteem

Our identity is our mental self-portrait. When we speak of our identity, we describe the person we see ourselves as being. On the other hand, when we speak about self-esteem we express our feeling about our mental self-portrait. This includes what we like and dislike about ourselves. Self-esteem development can increase narcissism; what we need is a godly self-concept.

Four Building Blocks of a Godly Self-Concept

According to the Griffin, "self-esteem (what I would call self-concept) is a firm wall of four separate building blocks, each as important as the others".[1]

The first building block is *a sense of moral worth*. For people to have high self-concept they must be confident that they are approved by God. They need the inner assurance that they will react in a good or upright way when confronted with an ethical choice.

The second building block is *a sense of competence*. Even though there is always room for improvement, we should all be confident that we are good at what we do. The

---

[1] From Em Griffin, Making Friends, Chapter 2, pp. 27-44

feeling of competence is only partially determined by our ability; the other factor is the level of our expectation. Self-esteem/concept rises if we either increase our skill or scale down our pretensions. The reverse is also true. We will become discouraged if expectation rises without an equal rise in competence.

The third building block of self-esteem is *a sense of self-determination*. Even though it may not be biblically true, the feelings of having control over ones' destiny has enabled many to accomplish their goals. A feeling of self-determination is crucial for a positive self-concept. Experientially, people who have a low view of themselves usually feel powerless to change their lives. They may see themselves as victims. Conversely, men and women with positive self-regard are willing to accept responsibility for their own lives. They feel like subjects rather than objects, actors as opposed to acted upon.

The final building block of self-esteem is *a sense of unity*. A sense of unity speaks of reliable, consistent behavior, "having it all together." Of course, like many, we often feel like we have it all together, while forgetting where we put it!

Several Characteristics of High Esteem People

There are several noticeable characteristics of people who have high self-esteem. First of all, they like themselves. They are essentially comfortable in their own skin. They are eager to participate and speak often with confidence. Self-doubt usually causes silence and withdrawal. Self-liking leads to participation.

People with a healthy self-image tend to be more spontaneous than those who look down on themselves. They are more likely to take risks in relationships.

People who feel good about themselves resist change for the sake of change (especially to please others). They are not easily persuaded. They find it easy to resist group pressure or ignore a persuasive appeal. Self-esteem and assertiveness are linked.

Those with high self-esteem are happy to be alive. The world looks good to them. Life seems basically positive. In their dealings with other people, they tend to mirror 1 Corinthians 13:7. They tend to bear all things, believe all things, hope all things, and endure all things.

People with high-self-esteem can handle criticism better than those who are down on themselves. They sift the words for possible help in doing a better job. They even get impatient with endless praise and flattery. They are looking for an honest, expert evaluation and are willing to take their lumps to get it.

So, what does this have to do with our identity in Christ? Well, my assumption is that a new creation in Christ who understands who they are in Christ will carry a godly self-concept and healthy self-esteem...a component of the abundant life Christ promised. (John 10:10)

"I would rather be what God chose to make me than the most glorious creature that I could think of; for to have been thought about, born in God's thought, and then made by God, is the dearest, grandest and most precious thing in all thinking."

— George MacDonald

Chapter Two:
Knowing Who We Are in Christ

In 2015, I had the great honor of preaching a series titled "Introduction to Identity: Is our life and world going to be better, worse, or the same?" I conducted this series at Fontana Christian Fellowship International Ministries, which is pastored by Gary, Gina, and Kalina Holley. The primary Scripture utilized for this series of messages begins with the book of Romans Chapter 8:1-36, which follows:

"Therefore, there is now no condemnation for those who are in Christ Jesus. For the law of the Spirit of life in Christ Jesus has set you free from the law of sin and of death. For what the Law could not do, weak as it was through the flesh, God did: sending His own Son in the likeness of sinful flesh and as an offering for sin, He condemned sin in the flesh, so that the requirement of the Law might be fulfilled in us, who do not walk according to the flesh but according to the Spirit. For those who are according to the flesh set their minds on the things of the flesh, but those who are according to the Spirit, the things of the Spirit. For the mind set on the flesh is death, but the mind set on the Spirit is life and peace, because the mind set on the flesh is hostile toward God; for it does not subject itself to the law of God, for it is not even able to do so, and those who are in the flesh cannot please God.

However, you are not in the flesh but in the Spirit, if indeed the Spirit of God dwells in you. But if anyone does not have the Spirit of Christ, he does not belong to

Him. If Christ is in you, though the body is dead because of sin, yet the spirit is alive because of righteousness. But if the Spirit of Him who raised Jesus from the dead dwells in you, He who raised Christ Jesus from the dead will also give life to your mortal bodies through His Spirit who dwells in you.

So then, brethren, we are under obligation, not to the flesh, to live according to the flesh— for if you are living according to the flesh, you must die; but if by the Spirit you are putting to death the deeds of the body, you will live. For all who are being led by the Spirit of God, these are sons of God. For you have not received a spirit of slavery leading to fear again, but you have received a spirit of adoption as sons by which we cry out, "Abba! Father!" The Spirit Himself testifies with our spirit that we are children of God, and if children, heirs also, heirs of God and fellow heirs with Christ, if indeed we suffer with Him so that we may also be glorified with Him.

For I consider that the sufferings of this present time are not worthy to be compared with the glory that is to be revealed to us. For the anxious longing of the creation waits eagerly for the revealing of the sons of God. For the creation was subjected to futility, not willingly, but because of Him who subjected it, in hope that the creation itself also will be set free from its slavery to corruption into the freedom of the glory of the children of God. For we know that the whole creation groans and suffers the pains of childbirth together until now. And not only this, but also we ourselves, having the first fruits of the Spirit, even we ourselves groan within ourselves, waiting eagerly for our adoption as sons, the redemption of our body. For in hope we have been saved, but hope that is seen is not hope; for who hopes for what he already sees? But if we hope for what we do not see, with perseverance we wait eagerly for it.

Our Victory in Christ

In the same way, the Spirit also helps our weakness; for we do not know how to pray as we should, but the Spirit Himself intercedes for us with groanings too deep for words; and He who searches the hearts knows what the mind of the Spirit is, because He intercedes for the saints according to the will of God.

And we know that God causes all things to work together for good to those who love God, to those who are called according to His purpose. For those whom He foreknew, He also predestined to become conformed to the image of His Son, so that He would be the firstborn among many brethren; and these whom He predestined, He also called; and these whom He called, He also justified; and these whom He justified, He also glorified.

What then shall we say to these things? If God is for us, who is against us? He who did not spare His own Son, but delivered Him over for us all, how will He not also with Him freely give us all things? Who will bring a charge against God's elect? God is the one who justifies; who is the one who condemns? Christ Jesus is He who died, yes, rather who was raised, who is at the right hand of God, who also intercedes for us. Who will separate us from the love of Christ? Will tribulation, or distress, or persecution, or famine, or nakedness, or peril, or sword? Just as it is written,

> *'FOR YOUR SAKE WE FACE DEATH ALL DAY LONG; WE ARE CONSIDERED AS SHEEP TO BE SLAUGHTERED.'*

But in all these things we overwhelmingly conquer through Him who loved us. For I am convinced that neither death, nor life, nor angels, nor principalities, nor things present, nor things to come, nor powers, nor height, nor depth, nor any other created thing, will be able to separate us from the love of God, which is in Christ Jesus our Lord."

As believers, we are not the same person now on a different path; we are a NEW creation. A brand-new person speaks of our purpose or our destiny, which bates the question, who are we? Especially in light of what the world says about us and what Scripture speaks regarding our relationship with God and one another, the question seems so very important…who are we really? Secondly, we must ask the question, where are we as individuals and corporately as a church regarding our identity and purpose in Christ? Again, in light of that question we must ask the follow up question, where are we going, or if you will, what is our focus as we move forward in the grace and presence of God.

"The ego is the false self-born out of fear and defensiveness."

— John O'Donohue, Anam Cara: A Book of Celtic Wisdom

Chapter Three:
Life Struggles

Perspectives

The struggles of life continue, regardless of how virtuous we try to live or not live; troubles seem to come in life. As I've evaluated my own life I see that most of my struggles come from three primary areas.

First, is my own unique stuff. We know that everyone has issues, sometimes stemming from our past, sometimes in our present and sometimes because of worries about the future. Regardless of where they come from, it's inherent that we as believers continuously work to deal with the stuff of life.

Secondly, my struggle, which seems to be common in the present day, is regarding religion versus freedom in Christ. For example, in the Old Testament, leprosy was a dreaded disease with no known cure. There were specific requirements which were placed upon a priest to deal with the fear of the spread of this dreaded disease. This was highly understandable given the knowledge that they had regarding the disease in that day, and the lack of appropriate treatment. Thus, it is assumed that, given the difficulty that one has in understanding a disease that seems to be incurable we should simply throw our hands up and assume the Old Testament stance of simply trying to protect ourselves from potential harm. In the New Testament, a different perspective is presented. That is the perspective of Christ himself, who would, when encountering lepers simply heal them by the grace of God and the power of the Holy Spirit. In my mind, I need to be, as the writer of Ephesians stated, trying to find out what pleases the Lord. What pleases him is living in the freedom for which Christ has made us free, not in the bondage of Old Testament rules, regulations, and shame. Christ was not ashamed of himself, the stories about him (virgin birth, right…run to Egypt, right, Nazareth, ah come on) nor of people that God created in his image and likeness, even if temporarily marred by sin, sickness, or disease.

Thirdly, and perhaps most profoundly are my fears. All of us have fears. Some fears are related to the past, some to the present, some to the future and some are simply irrational fears that we've held onto since childhood. I know my mind needs to be renewed, as presented by Paul the Apostle in Romans Chapter 12. For right-thinking leads to right living. But of course, it starts with knowing who we are.

Context is the Key

In the book of Romans, Paul is writing to a blended church made up of both Jew and Gentile. Overall, this church was one formerly rooted in paganism, where excess is best, and they experienced grave fears regarding principalities and powers, i.e. Satanic powers, and many superstitions. They struggled with who they were in light of false teaching that had come to them out of Jerusalem. Historically, the church in Rome was a Jewish expression made up of Jews who had settled in Rome primarily for business purposes, but had come to faith in Christ. In a time of persecution by the Roman Emperor of the day, the Jews had been forced to leave, including Messianic Jews, most of which would've returned to Jerusalem or Judea as a place of respite until they could return to Rome. Thus, the church in Rome that remained became primarily a Gentile church. A few years passed, and the Jews returned to Rome and came with their teaching that stated in order to be a good Christian or follower of Christ one had to embrace fully Jewish traditions, including sacrifices, visiting the Temple, and practicing various rituals that were part of the Jewish culture of the day. Thus, Paul was writing to this church to clarify for them and to correct this teaching so that the Gentile believers did not come under the same bondage that was often experienced by those who embraced the Jewish viewpoint of Christianity.

Utilizing Paul's teaching in the letter to the church in Rome, as well as other scriptures, we will look at identity. As we begin, it is helpful to remember that Paul never told people what to do until he first told them who they were. This applied to saints and sinners alike. So, lets launch.

No Condemnation

Romans eight starts out with this wonderful, phenomenal statement, "There is therefore now no condemnation for those in Christ Jesus." We are not condemned! Those of us in Christ have been set free from the law of sin and death, which brings us under the law of Christ! What? Grace brings us into the law of the spirit of life in Christ Jesus. The law of sin and death is no longer a law we even consider. It is dead, according to Paul, as are we. Those who live according to the flesh (speaking more about ego, or selfishness than our physical existence) shall naturally live according to fleshly (worldly or natural) principles, as do those who have the law of the spirit living in their lives.

Naturally...that is, it is natural for those that live a life of the Spirit to do so from the awareness and activation of God's presence in their life. But for those who naturally serve the flesh, of course they will naturally serve their flesh. Thus, we are to live from a place of total freedom, naturally, that is, from the new nature that lives in us...which is of course a bit easier said than done. In spite of this wonderful revelation, that we are free from the law, choices still remain.

"Therefore if you have been raised up with Christ, keep seeking the things above, where Christ is, seated at the right hand of God. Set your mind on the things above, not on the things that are on earth. For you have died and your life is hidden with Christ in God. When Christ, who is our life, is revealed, then you also will be revealed with Him in glory. Therefore consider the members of your earthly body as dead to immorality, impurity, passion, evil desire, and greed, which amounts to idolatry. For it is because of these things that the wrath of God will come upon the sons of disobedience, and in them you also once walked, when you were living in them. But now you also, put them all aside: anger, wrath, malice, slander, and abusive speech from your mouth. Do not lie to one another, since you laid aside the old self with its evil practices, and have put on the new self who is being renewed to a true knowledge according to the image of the One who created him--a renewal in which there is no distinction between Greek and Jew, circumcised and uncircumcised, barbarian, Scythian, slave and freeman, but Christ is all, and in all. So, as those who have been chosen of God, holy and beloved, put on a heart of compassion, kindness, humility, gentleness and pa-

tience; bearing with one another, and forgiving each other, whoever has a complaint against anyone; just as the Lord forgave you, so also should you. Beyond all these things put on love, which is the perfect bond of unity." (Colossians 3:1-14)

This reminds us, as seen in Colossians 3, but in other passages as well that we are to set our minds on the things that are above, not focused on the continuous troubles in the earth. That is, focusing on the Spirit. Life and peace are indeed key to a successful life in God. So, you have flesh but you are not flesh: remember, remember, remember, you are in the spirit and the Spirit is in you. Plus, you are now and moving forward as righteous, sin free, un-condemned, loved, and chosen...fellow heirs with Christ.

What does this mean for us believers as we move forward in this century? Well, for me, and many others, who have lived a life of performance orientation designed to win God's (or mom and dad's) approval, I need to let go of the notion of fixing me through the flesh (self-effort, self-help, self, self, self).

However, I do need to renew my mind, and each day present myself to the Lord as a living sacrifice as it states in Romans chapter 12. This is a holy act. It is reasonable, makes perfect sense and is true worship of the Lord. So, we set our minds on God with the knowledge that he will daily renew our minds so that we think more and more like him.

Since we know who we are, the righteousness of God in Christ, a New Creation in him, the head, not the tail, we must act like it. That is, like putting on a brand-new coat that has been perfectly tailored to our body, we put on Christ and forget about what we used to be, what we used to wear, how we used to act. We are not a new person in Christ in the same old house, if you will, or a better version of our old self. We are truly brand new and getting better!

But how can this be, or how does this happen for me? It is all grace, grace, grace…and the working of the Lord in our lives, with a little bit of help from God's friend…us!

In Philippians chapter 2 verses 12 and 13, Paul the apostle writes,

> " Therefore, my beloved, as you have always obeyed, so now not only as in my presence but much more in my absence, work out your own salvation with fear and trembling, for it is God who works in you both to will and to work for his good pleasure."

What a wonderful promise this is for all believers. Even if we are thoroughly convinced of our identity in Christ, firmly and completely confident, with absolute assurance of his goodness and grace for our lives, we still have stuff to work on. All of us do, for all of our lives. The good news is, God's word is working out a plan in us; it's a plan to bring pleasure to him and Shalom (goodness, blessing, peace, and prosperity) for us. Of course, we must work, for we are responsible for our own salvation, but he is also working in us each day by his wonderful grace, helping us to become everything we already are in Christ through his finished work of the cross, his ascension, his enthronement at the right hand of the Father and the outpouring of the Holy Spirit. Remember, we are seated with him in heavenly places. (Ephesians 2:6)

And such were some of you.

Who am I really? Let us remember, as believers, we are not the same person now on a different path. We are a new creation on a new path. Path always speaks of our purpose or our destiny; it speaks of the direction that we are going and as believers, we know that God is in charge, as we allow him to be Lord of our lives. Sometimes in order to reach one's destiny or purpose there are things that need to be forgotten, and there are things that need to be embraced. Knowing the difference is the real key to success in our walk in God.

Our perspective, 1 Corinthians chapter 6 verses 9 through 11,

> *"Or do you not know that the unrighteous will not inherit the kingdom of God? Do not be deceived; neither fornicators, nor idolaters, nor adulterers, nor effeminate, nor homosexuals, nor thieves, nor the covetous, nor drunkards, nor revilers, nor swindlers, will inherit the kingdom of God. And such were some of you."*

Well, so much for good news! But... Then Paul goes on to say,

> *"but you were washed, but you were sanctified, but you were justified in the name of the Lord Jesus Christ and in the Spirit of our God".*

What a big, beautiful difference that is! If one were to only read the first part of this passage it would be very easy to become discouraged. Which one of us has not at best been covetous toward something or thought in our hearts about somebody else that does not belong to us. Praise God, because of the precious grace of God and the wonderful blood of Jesus, we have been washed (this is past tense), we have been saved (past, present and future), we were justified (again, past tense). In other words, no matter what we were, or what others think we were or are, from God's perspective we are all brothers and sisters, washed, cleansed, righteous, loved. Frankly, it is God's perspective that matters most.

God's Perspective

It is the precondition of all human beings that we tend toward being self-absorbed. I don't mean that we are by nature narcissistic, though all children start that way, but our general concern daily happens to be number one, that is ourselves. Much of what it means to grow up, to mature, to be transformed, is seen in our ability to move from self-absorption to being God and other focused. In many ways, this could be the best definition of God's love toward us, found in the Greek word agape, in that his focus is not on himself and his own satisfaction, but on his Word, his people, and his mission.

Gaining God's perspective on who we are is extremely important in the development of our overall identity as full and complete human beings. Thus, it's important for us to review how God does see us and where we fit into the grand scheme of the universe. My hope is that then we can proceed to a more well-rounded understanding our position in Christ, our authority in him and the purpose for which we have been called.

In the book of Ephesians chapter 1, beginning in verse one, we read,

"Paul, an apostle of Christ Jesus by the will of God, to the saints who are in Ephesus, who were faithful in Christ Jesus. Grace to you and peace from God our father and the Lord Jesus Christ. Blessed be the God and father of our Lord Jesus Christ who has blessed us with every spiritual blessing in the heavenlies in Christ just as he chose us in him before the foundation of the world that we should be holy and blameless before him. In love he predestined us to adoption as sons through Jesus Christ to himself, according to be in the kind intention of his will."

What a wonderful passage of Scripture written under the inspiration of the Holy Spirit by Paul the Apostle. In this passage Paul makes several very important declarations that speak to the main part of this study

First of all, unlike many people today, Paul does not call us sinners saved by grace, but in fact calls us saints. Because of God's wonderful grace we receive the peace of God because we've experienced the forgiveness of sin. Thus, we have every possible blessing provided to us in Christ. In fact, from the very foundation of the world we were chosen to be a part of God's family. This simply means that regardless of our natural birth, we can stand in absolute confidence, knowing that we are not a mistake of biology, but that in fact we were fully and completely chosen by God from before time began. Not only were we chosen, but he predetermined that those that believe in Christ and serve him with a whole heart will be completely conformed to the very image of Christ. That does not mean we will lose our unique personality, but will begin to think, act, and even feel more and more like Jesus day by day. We will be like him and not just when we get to heaven, but here and now, day by day. Remember, it is his will that we grow from childhood (John 1:12) to Sonship, or through adoption (Romans 8: 14-17). Frankly, the highest status any of us can have as believers is not Apostle, Prophet, Pastor, or even President, but to be called Son...not THE son of God, but A son of God...simply because we have been adopted by him for his purposes.

We have been invited into the divine love story of God. God the Father, God the Son and God the Holy Spirit have invited us into their unique dance of love. What an incredible blessing given to each of us. Yet many have not experienced the gift that is provided to us through Christ, redemption on the cross. As it states in many passages, mankind is without true excuse, for the law of sin and death still operates in their lives. But for those of us liberated by Christ, the law of sin and death is no longer even to be considered. When Christ died, we died, and are dead to our trespasses and sin. When he was buried, we were buried, symbolized in our baptism in water. When he was raised, we were raised, and the resurrection power of Christ lives in us. When he ascended, we ascended and when he was seated in power and glory, so were we, at the right hand of the Father in heaven. We are presently in a position of incredible majesty provided to us because of all that Christ has done for us.

What Paul wants us to see and what I'm asking you to consider is what an exalted position we have in Christ. As stated in Second Corinthians 5:17, we are a new creation. The word "new" in this passage is the word (kainos), which means recently made, fresh, recent, unused, unworn and as respects substance of a new kind, unprecedented, novel, uncommon, unheard of.

The old has passed away and has become new, which invites us to question what has passed away and what has become new. What has passed away is our sin nature through the work of Christ' death on the cross, which allows for the forgiveness of sin. What is new is that we are fully alive in Christ, that is, we are filled with light and life; resurrection life. We are now dead to sin, according to Romans 6:12, and alive in Christ. As one of my dear pastoral friends likes to say when asked how he is, he states "I am well and good by God's grace and getting better." And he means this, that every day, by God's grace, he is getting better and better. That is the case for all of us who are in Christ.

The Grand Process

Based upon the finished work of Christ on the cross we can live truly and completely exchanged lives, as presented in Galatians 2:20.

> *"I have been crucified with Christ. It is no longer I who live, but Christ who lives in me. And the life I now live in the flesh I live by faith in the Son of God, who loved me and gave himself for me."*

We are essentially cold dead in Christ. Just to reiterate, remember that when he died we died, when he was buried, we were buried in him, when he was raised we were raised, when he ascended, in Christ we ascended with him, and now we are seated with him in the heavenlies, at the right hand of the Father. Thus, as believers we must stop and ponder for a moment what royalty, what dignity, what grandeur we share with our Risen Lord, and learn to walk differently since we have received all blessings due to what Christ has done for us. That is, Christ has made every provision for us through his resurrection power that raised him from the dead and has given us the fullness of life.

Once again, contemplate for a moment, what does Christ's provision and power provide to us? First, it provides his unique, creative love, as we are filled with the Holy Spirit, which allows for his fruit to be manifested in our lives. We have been gifted by the Holy Spirit, enabled by his grace, for we believe fully what he has said about us. This is summarized in many areas of the New Testament, especially in the letters of Paul, but also of John. First let us look at the book of Colossians, beginning with chapter 1 verses 13-14.

> *"For He rescued us from the domain of darkness, and transferred us to the kingdom of His beloved Son, in whom we have redemption, the forgiveness of sins."*

To continue with these thoughts, several other passages may be cited, but are simply summarized here. For example, we have been redeemed; forgiven from all of our sins. Colossians 1:27 simply states that Christ is in me, and of course we are in him. Further, Colossians 2:7 states that since we are firmly rooted in Christ, we are now being built up in him and have been made complete in Christ. According to Colossians 2:10, we are to remember it is through Jesus exchanged life (Colossians 2:12, 13) that we've been buried and made alive with Christ. What a glorious reality that is for each of us. Colossians 3: 1-4 states we are raised up with Christ, and in 1 John 4:17 we read that as Jesus is, so are we in this world.

Thus, we have not been given a spirit of fear but of power, of love and of a sound mind (2 Timothy 1:7). Further, we have been saved and called for a divine purpose, by God's grace. We can never say with conviction that we are not worth much, as we are worth everything to the Father (2 Timothy 1:9). His saving us was not because we needed his mercy...which we do, and have received, fully and completely in Christ. (Titus 3:5) His saving us was because of his wonderful grace.

In Hebrews 2:11 we read that we are sanctified (set apart to God) because Christ is our sanctifier, and he has done so for a grand and glorious purpose. He is not ashamed to call us his brother or sister...he is proud of each of us. Of course, the difficulty for most believers is believing that what is said in scripture is true for us; that all the Word of God has declared about us is true. If it is indeed true, Hebrews 4:16 becomes easy for us, for we know that we can come boldly before the very throne of God to find mercy and grace in time of need. Frankly, how far away is the Father from us? If in spiritual reality we are seated in the heavenlies with Christ, ask yourself, where is Christ? Is he not seated at the right hand of the Father in glory? And are we not seated with him, according to the inspired writings of the Apostle? If that is truly true, then the Father is easily accessible to us for he is right next to us...He is seated on his throne and we are seated in the very lap of Christ. Thus, without effort, we can easily turn our hearts and minds towards the Father, knowing that his face is turned toward us, and always toward his Son.

Thusly postured, we can come before the Lord, and bring our concerns, our dreams, our needs, which he already knows before we ever ask, and he hears and responds. We have already received exceedingly great and precious promises through God, since we are partakers of the very nature of God.

So, what does that mean for us? What we need today more than anything else is believing believers, rather than unbelieving believers. By faith we need to declare the truth and then act upon it. As he lives, so are we in this world! (1John 4:17) This is the key Scripture that we will look at as we continue to move forward in our study.

By this, love is perfected with us, so that we may have confidence in the day of judgment; because as He is, so also are we in this world.

John the Apostle, 1 John 4:17

Chapter Four:
Identity

As He is, so are We in this World

I remember a while back singing a fairly popular chorus with a line that says, "there is none like you." In many ways, this is a true statement. For God is the creator and sustainer of all things, and is holy and righteous and just. But according to Scripture the statement isn't totally true. In fact, there are a lot of folks like God, for in Christ, we are a new creation, and daily we are being conformed into the image of Christ. Thus, in fact, God has declared that we are like him. Now when I sing the song, I add the little phrase, there is none like you…except me.

In this section, the focus will be on who we are from a biblical perspective. Much of this material has been gleaned from the wonderful work of Dr. Barry Chant, the younger brother of the Vision International College founder Dr. Ken Chant. I am very appreciative for the exceptional book that Dr. Barry has written, and with permission have taken some of his major points and expanded on them.[2]

The Bible says that each one of us were created, not begotten. Only Jesus was begotten. We are truly unique, one-of-a-kind, equal, and yet one of billions. In Genesis chapter 1 verses 26 to 28 the Bible says we were created in his image and his likeness, and that we would have

---

[2] Barry Chant, Living in the Image of God, Barry Chant Ministries

dominion over everything else that God had created. Our dominion was not to extend to each other, for human beings were never to lord it over or dominate each other, only over the rest of the created order.

We are able to rule with justice because we have the ability to think like our creator; creatively; comprehensively. We can see things the way God sees them, as the writer John wrote, as he is (that is, Jesus) so are we in this world. We are a spirit with a soul in a body. The spirit is the lamp of the Lord, according to Psalm 21:2, and it is the spirit and soul that return to the Lord when we die. (Ecclesiastes 12:7) Eventually, our body will decay, but our spirit grows stronger and stronger each day (1 Thessalonians 5:23). It is through our soul we are able to communicate with each other and with God, as our soul expresses our thoughts, feelings, and intentions. Without a doubt, we are fearfully and wonderfully made. Thus...

We are of infinite value

We are of infinite value, not just to each other, but most importantly to God. Our worth to God was demonstrated by the incarnation of Christ, leading to Jesus death, burial, and resurrection. The Bible says we were bought and paid for as men and women, redeemed by the very precious blood of Jesus himself. (1Peter 1:18 and 19) Considering all God has done for us, it would be helpful to take some time to remember some of the statements in Scripture that speak about how unique, special and precious we are to God. We can do this under the title, who am I?

WHO AM I?

The Scripture says that I am the salt of the earth, I am the light of the world, I am child of God, a part of the true vine, and a channel of the grace of God. I am Christ's friend and have been chosen and called by Christ to bear fruit and fruit that remains. I am what I am the Apostle Paul declared about himself. He also stated he was a slave to righteousness, enslaved to God as a son of God, for God is our Father, and we are heirs of God and joint heirs with Christ, sharing in the wonderful inheritance provided to us by our faith in him.

Further I am a Temple in which God's Spirit dwells or lives, and I am joined to the Lord, one in spirit with him. Thus, I am a member of Christ's body, a new creation, reconciled to God and a minister of reconciliation. I am a fellow free citizen with the rest of God's people, in his family and yet I can also state clearly that I am a prisoner of Christ, and only righteous and holy because of all that he has done for me. This makes me a citizen of heaven and at the very present I am seated in the heavenlies with Christ at the right hand of the Father. As such, I am an expression of the life of Christ because he is my life. I have been chosen of God, holy, beloved, not in the future but in the present and his presence. I am one of God's living stones, being built up in Christ as a part of a spiritual house, part of God's chosen race, a royal priesthood, a holy nation. I am God's own possession, no longer an alien and a stranger. In so many ways I am undeserving of the wonderful love and grace given through Christ, Yet I must state clearly, by the grace of God I am not the great I AM, but by the grace of God I am what I am and honestly this is all the opinion that matters. It is vitally important as believers that we continue to renew our minds, and we do so by no longer remembering all the sin that we've done. Being sin conscious does not give glory to God, or benefit us in the least, but we must continually focus our attention on all that God has done in and through us, becoming God conscious, and agreeing with all and every declaration of God concerning us. When we as believers begin to agree in thought and action with all God says we are, we will manifest his character for the world to see, giving glory to God.

As He is 2

After I wrote the last chapter, I got pretty excited. It was not because of the brilliance of my insights, it was the very thought of all that we have and all we are right now in Christ. In another one of my books, Grace and Truth, I focus much of my attention on this wonderful dual blessing, because as Jesus is, so are we, or at least should/could be; full of grace and truth. One aspect of truth, which is relational not simply propositional, is that truth is an expression of beauty. In Genesis when God created man, he said that his creation was very good. Good in the Hebrew language is often interpreted as beautiful. That is why it is somewhat interesting that the immediate effect of sin was for the man and woman to try and hide themselves from God, as though they were no longer beautiful. Obviously, they were embarrassed and guilty, but instead of standing tall before God who created them and loved them, they shrank away into the shadows, attempting to hide themselves from God who sees and knows everything. In other words, they no longer could see themselves as God did. God intended us to see ourselves as worthwhile, valuable creatures who have no need to be ashamed. The good news of the kingdom of God is that we are already beautiful in the eyes of God, becoming more so day by day. We are God's masterpiece, as scripture states in Ephesians 2:10.

"We are his workmanship, created in Christ Jesus for good works, which God prepared beforehand, that we should walk in them."

Without question we are God's greatest work of art.

I love sitting on my patio at home, enjoying the view that my location provides. From my hilltop vantage point, I can see the mountains, the valley below and at night I often have a spectacular view of the stars above. As beautiful as all of this is, it doesn't compare to the beauty of a child; the beauty of any man or woman created in the image of God. We are truly God's masterpiece and though sin disfigured that masterpiece, we are not less in the eyes of God. We may be less in the eyes of each other, but not in God's.

In the scripture just quoted, the word created draws attention to the reality that when we come to Christ, the image of God is renewed in each of us. The good works we have been created for are God works, work that is beyond our natural ability to accomplish, but by his empowerment, through the gifts he provides us, we certainly can fulfill his purpose as a part of his continuing masterpiece.

More in Ephesians

In the first three chapters of Ephesians, brilliant Paul the Apostle summarizes all that God has done for us. In chapter 1 of Ephesians, Paul addresses the church in the city of Ephesus as saints. A saint is someone who was been made holy by God. Holy signifies that they've been set aside for God's wonderful purpose. Paul continues to say that we are rich because we've been blessed. The word blessed in the Greek comes from a verb "eulogeo" which means to speak well of and to have favor. God has completely and fully blessed us to be able to accomplish whatever task we have been given. It's important to remember that every blessing is already ours. Nothing needs to be added in terms of God's favor or grace for us. We need not strive to please God, or to bless him, for he is already pleased with us, and we already bless his heart. Of course, when we act in less than who we are fashioned to be, less than loving to others, not particularly faithful in our service, it displeases the Father, just as it would displease any natural mother or father to see one of their children acting in a way that is not as much of what they are capable of. Scripture clearly states that we are complete in Christ, not working in that direction. We are alive and well upon coming to Christ.

Therefore, we know that God has blessed us with every spiritual blessing, including the fact that he chose us, predestined us, adopted us, redeemed us, and forgave us. We are lavished with his grace upon us and he has made known to us the mysteries of God, all because we are a chip off the old block... We are a lot like him. We are sealed by the Holy Spirit and we have an inheritance provided to us through Jesus death, burial, and resurrection. He is always with us wherever we go. We are members of his royal family and heirs of the King.

Unfortunately, the vast majority of the body of Christ are ignorant of these wonderful promises. The truth is, we don't have to work or struggle to obtain the specialized state of holiness or righteousness whereby we gain access to the love and blessings of God. No, sorry, you have it right now. Because we are in him, and thus we are like him, it's only natural for us (well perhaps supernatural) to want to be more like him day by day. Thus, we may well ask ourselves the question, what kinds of changes do I need to make in my life to be more of who I already am? What will it cost? What am I willing to give up or go after? As we develop the long list of do's and don'ts, we begin a battle between should I or shouldn't I, can I or can't I, should I obey or do my own thing, leading to a failure to believe that we can ever be fully all that we've been created to be in Christ. A lack of faith keeps many believers from acting as though they already are filled with the love of God, filled with the grace of God, filled with the power of God. In other words, fully God's person. In our exertion and exhaustive attempt to become, we never achieve what we hope to, to be fully kingdom people, full of righteousness, peace, and joy.

But, and this is a big but, if we can grasp the fullness of this revelation of who we are in Christ, we can then grasp what Paul hoped would be the results of us fully knowing this revelation, the mystery that should not be a mystery to us as believers. The first principle Paul hopes we grasp is that we would know the hope to which we have been called. What is that hope? The hope is that everything that has been declared in God's word is truly ours, and secondly, he wanted us to know the riches of his glorious inheritance of the saints. What is our inheritance? Again, it's everything that God has promised us within his word. Finally, he wants the church to know the incomparably great power that is provided to all of us who believe.

We know according to Scripture that Christ was exalted above every power in heaven and on earth…he is King of kings and Lord of lords. He was lifted up over every spiritual entity and authority. Even today there are powerful people and ideas that attempt to lord it over the church and his people. The word for lord is Arche, from which we get the word for Archbishop, meaning that which is above others. In other words, no matter who comes first, Christ is the head of all. Further, the word dunamis is where we get the word dynamite or Dynamo, speaking of the resurrection power of Christ which lives within each of us. In the spiritual sense, every spirit, every demonic power, every sin, every transgression, every evil tendency is under the authority of Christ and therefore under our authority as well. These are incredible truths. We must learn to recognize this as our present-day reality.

Paul Gives Us More

We move on to Paul's second great prayer in the third chapter of the book of Ephesians. The prayer, in summary, asks the Lord that we be strengthened with the power of the Holy Spirit, knowing that Christ dwells within us and that we will be fully established in his love, so much so that we know the full extent of Christ's love (measureless) and be filled with all the goodness of God.

God is great. His powers are immeasurable and his presence is always with us. So, what does this mean for us? God is able to do what we ask; he is able to do all we ask; he is able to do all we ask or imagine; he is able to do more than all that we ask or imagine; he is able to do immeasurably more than all we ask or even imagine. Wow...God is truly great!

What God has already done for us makes it possible for us to live without continuous struggle to become what we assume he wants us to be (and all that we do not measure up to). In Truth, I can simply allow the blessings of God to work out through my life. One must remember that if I've already been forgiven, blessed, adopted, graced, chosen, made alive, seated in heavenly places, and so on, then I can live in light of this reality. In other words, I become in practice, in Christ, who I already am.

But What About Now?

I can almost hear the naysayers. This is just too good to be true. The truth remains, as he is, so are we in this world. That doesn't mean that troubles won't visit us now and then, or that disappointments won't come our way. However, we can embrace by faith a new image of ourselves, that regardless the circumstances or situations of life, I am, now, everything that God has said that I am in Christ. This takes some practice. Certainly, it takes a sanctified imagination and the faith to act on what we know from God's word is true.

Again, Jesus did say in this world there would be trouble. Without a doubt, there is trouble in this life, and the troubler of this world is still alive and well...well alive anyway, and still seeks to rob, kill, and destroy.

There were many believers that struggle with the thought that they are supposed to live a victorious life in Christ. Supposed to, absolutely, because Christ is the one who was victorious, and he's in us, and we are in him. Thus, we are to live in victory over Satan and his works, a clear promise to all believers (Romans 8:37; 1 Corinthians 15:57; 2 Corinthians 2:14; 1 John 4:4). According to Scripture demons are subject to the very name of Jesus (see Luke 10:17-18). We share the same authority of Christ over the enemy (Luke 10:19 and Ephesians 1:22).

Undeniably, the enemy is trying to seduce people into idolatry, sorcery, and occultism, and convince people that sins of the flesh (ego or self) are also caused by the devil, with the hope of making us powerless to combat his power. Though people may well choose to walk in rebellion and some will even yield their lives to the devil, he has much less power than is often assumed in the church. In the culture where Paul lived worked and wrote, virtually everybody was an idol worshiper. Undoubtedly demonic activity existed as seen in the story of the Seven Sons of Sceva.

However, the New Testament writings, other than the gospels, had an emphasis on preaching and teaching, with salvation and growing in the Word and Spirit the goal. The apostles seemed to be less caught up in the customs of the day, nor were they concerned about overcoming demons and offering deliverance in their day. Their focus was on repentance and faith in Christ, because they recognized that, since Christ was already victorious, what one really needed was the Spirit of God living in them and the rest of the problems of life would take care of themselves.

Lust is not recorded in the bible as having its origin in demons, nor did expelling demons bring about deliverance from such things as pride, gluttony, bitterness, anger, greed, and fear. These are all defined as works of the flesh and are to be overcome by being washed and justified through faith in the name of Jesus and by being filled with the Holy Spirit. The risk of seeking release from the human conditions (sin) rather than the unquestionably harder process of discipleship, may be a way of avoiding responsibility for our growth in God. Growth in God is living life from the place of the finished work of Christ.... Christ in us, the hope of glory.

Depending on one's church background, it is difficult at times to grasp the true freedom we have in Christ provided by grace alone. Remember, scripture consistently reaffirms our freedom in Christ. That does not mean that demons are not around and active. I am certain they still are. But again, our focus is not to be sin, to be conscious of our mistakes or even willful disobedience. We are to be aware, but not to obsess. Instead, we are to be increasingly more Christ conscious, putting our daily trust in the goodness of God, his forgiveness, compassion, love. According to scripture, Christ disarmed, made a public display of the leaders of evil (Principalities and Powers), and has given us authority over them, an authority that requires our implementation for us to become powerful over the powers. Christ is now seated at the right hand of God in our lives, and we are co-residents with him, far above the enemy. We are no longer under the dominion of the devil. We can, by the grace of God and the power of his name avoid being led astray by them any longer. Although the devil does have the power to deceive, the same power he possessed in the Garden (and that is a powerful power), because we have the mind of Christ, it is difficult for the devil to persuade a mind focused upon Christ. Again, our focus is not on what the devil is or isn't doing, what his strategies are. We are not to be ignorant of his strategies, but we are to be steadfastly focused on fulfilling the mandate that God has given us. That is to live a life of compassion, sharing the good news of the kingdom of God and allowing the compassionate love of Christ to infect others for the glory of God.

As compassionate people of God we are motivated to share with people about the importance of relationship with our Father. Compassion moves us as it did Jesus in his ministry to the leper and the woman caught in adultery. Rather than judging, Jesus ministered his grace, knowing that they were living beneath who they really were as human beings. Loving compassion requires action, action that leads us to forgiving others while we are also experiencing God's forgiveness, and working toward justice by showing mercy and kindness. In other words, we are living out the complete image of God as true compassionate, loving, forgiving men and women who have been transformed by the wonderful and marvelous grace of God.

I am Like Him

There is a chorus with the phrase "there is none like you" …which is true, at least partially. It is true that God is above us, he is perfect in love, holiness, purpose, etc. But the statement is not entirely true, for the truth is, I am like him. And so are you. If you are in Christ and he is in you, which is truth, then in fact we are like him. But we are not alone in being like him. We have hundreds of thousands of millions of others who are also New Testament saints, who have been washed in the precious blood of Jesus, who have Holy Spirit, and are now part of the Church of Jesus Christ. We are all like him, for scripture declares that as many as received Christ, have become children of God…we are. Not will or if we pray and fast enough just might become…we are. We are a chip off the old block!

It is interesting to note that the emphasis of Jesus's ministry was not on the church, for he only preached about the church once. His emphasis was on the kingdom of God, or the rule of God over everything everywhere. Some would indicate that the church and the kingdom are essentially the same, but in fact they are quite distinct though related. The kingdom expands from heaven to earth and all points in between. That is why we pray your kingdom, and your will be done on earth as it is in heaven. The church is the gathering place for men and women to be nurtured, loved, trained, or equipped, corrected as required, so that together we can be an expression of God's grace as ambassadors in the world, declaring God's goodness, that his mercy endures forever. He is our King and is worthy to be praised.

In the New Testament, there is a clear distinction between all the people who lived in a city and the citizens of that city. It was only the citizens, either born citizens or made citizens (Freedman) who could be a part of the assembly, (ecclesia), making decisions on behalf of the larger community. Citizens of the Kingdom were called upon to develop plans of action to make sure smooth running of the whole community. Just as the crowd only becomes an assembly when gathered together, so it is with the church, which is only really the church when it is meeting. Thus, the church that was talked about in the New Testament is the local church. It's a congregation consisting of men and women who gather, pray, and worship, enjoy the sacraments such as the Lord's supper, and experience the blessing of true fellowship (koinonia) together. It is in this setting called the church that we can receive pastoral care, hear dynamic preaching, the reading of Scripture, reciting of prayers, times of worship and singing, within a dynamic community charged with the presence of God. The concept of a universal church is hardly known within Scripture.

In the body of Christ, all of us are one in him, because there's only one Spirit, one Lord, one faith, one baptism in one God and Father of all. (Ephesians 4:4-6) The local church is, if you will, the microcosm of the universal church, made up of all believers everywhere. It is in the local churches that we learn who we really are. It is here that our spiritual identity is formed and in some cases deformed, depending upon what we are taught about ourselves. We are all members of the local church, designed for dynamic fellowship, and the scriptures provide several pictures of how this local church can function. These include analogies such as a body, a temple, a household, a garden, and a bride. However, it is of the metaphor of the family that provides the best picture of what God intends for his dynamic church.

In a family, there are certain rights and privileges, along with definite responsibilities, assuming it is a semi functional family. As members, we choose, well somewhat choose, to be obedient to the leaders of the home, and embrace our responsibilities through discipline. There's an orderliness along with shared resources and leadership found within family life, that should also be modeled in the church. Why is the church so important? Because Jesus said he would build his church and not even hell itself can stop it. Just like in our families, it is in the local church we learn to be a member of the family of God, becoming molded into the image of the parents God has given. In similar fashion, in the local church Christ is formed in us, as we submit to the discipline of worship, prayer, bible study and service. In the church is where we hopefully learn who we really are in Christ and are encouraged to become everything he created us to be.

Children-Young Men-Fathers

In our pursuit of identity, people pass through various stages. From a natural view, theorists such as Erickson, Piaget, even Freud taught the progression of human development over time. These concepts are not new, but echo the teaching of John the Apostle in 1 John 2:12-14.

> *"I am writing to you, little children, because your sins have been forgiven you for His name's sake. I am writing to you, fathers, because you know Him who has been from the beginning. I am writing to you, young men, because you have overcome the evil one. I have written to you, children, because you know the Father. I have written to you, fathers, because you know Him who has been from the beginning. I have written to you, young men, because you are strong, and the word of God abides in you, and you have overcome the evil one."*

In my book, *Journey to Wholeness,* I expound on this scripture in detail. Without repeating my previous writing, the scripture remains germane to our discussion on identity. We all start our journey in life as children. Children are not Tabla Rosa, a blank slate that the world writes upon, but in fact enters the world with a consistent through life personality focus, general temperament, etc. This temperament or personality is modified over time through the interaction with the world (parents, school, church, etc.). As observed, children are innocent, vulnerable, easily influenced by authority figures, dependent on caregivers, etc. Of course, they are fully human at birth, and grow in their humanity over time.

In a similar sense, when we are born from above (John 3) we are, as described by Paul, a new creation, and are fully alive in Christ, fully spiritual. We must grow into the fullness of our spiritual potential, known only to God, over time. As children, we are also vulnerable, dependent on caregivers in the church, easily influenced by authority figures, etc., requiring loving, nurturing and protection as we grow in God. A strong foundation of faith is needed (trust) to grow to maturity.

In time, as we grow in family, face obstacles from the enemy, deal with our own inner conflict and the world, we have choices. Our choice in dealing with life is often to run, hide or take on more responsibility, and work through our past. We become "young men" through the study of the Word and facing truth with grace...overcoming the evil one. However, we don't stop at learning to overcome and becoming strong through the Word of God, but we are to continue to full...

Sonship thorough Adoption

This is what John the Apostle is presenting in the concept of Fathers...mature believers who know God by experience. They are true sons of God, who have been trained to think and act like the Father, and thus can be trusted by the Father to act in his behalf. In our present-day madness over titles and accolades designed to define us or at least affirm our worth, men especially, but women are not exempt, settling for simple sonship seems almost insulting. We often long for the superior gifts, such as apostle or prophet, or honorific titles such as bishop or archbishop (and I suppose someday we will have a Pope of Pentecost!). In Jesus day, as seen in his baptism, the highest honor, the most grand and glorious title one could have was that of Son. Of course, we are not THE Son of God, but in Christ, as New Creation, we are sons of God, and wherever we are in our journey, child, young man, or emerging father, we are sons, and become all God has created us to be. We have infinite worth in the eyes of our Creator, and we should remember that every human is loved, worthwhile, and has an eternal destiny.

I am who the Father says that I am…and I will be all that he wants me to be as I yield my life to him in obedient fellowship, in him and in the church.

Epilogue

Throughout scripture, and history for that matter, transformation of men's and women's character leading to a new (or perhaps re-discovered) identity formation can be seen. Having preached this series of messages for Fontana Christian Fellowship Internationals Ministries, and several other congregations, it is germane to reference and briefly discuss some of these biblical characters that have influenced and illustrate my thinking. Here are three from the Old Testament, and three from the New Testament...and I could have chosen many more, but these I believe will suffice.

In Genesis 32: 24-31 we read;

> *"Then Jacob was left alone, and a man wrestled with him until daybreak. When he saw that he had not prevailed against him, he touched the socket of his thigh; so the socket of Jacob's thigh was dislocated while he wrestled with him. Then he said, "Let me go, for the dawn is breaking." But he said, "I will not let you go unless *you bless me."So he said to him, "What is your name?" And he said, "Jacob."He said, "Your name shall no longer be Jacob, but Israel; for you have striven with God and with men and have prevailed." Then Jacob asked him and said, "Please tell me your name." But he said, "Why is it that you ask my name?" And he blessed him there. So Jacob named * the place Peniel, for he said, "I have seen God face to face, yet my life has been preserved." Now the sun rose*

*upon him just as he crossed over Penuel, and he
was limping on his thigh. Therefore *, to this day
the sons of Israel do not eat the sinew of the hip
which is on the socket of the thigh, because he
touched the socket of Jacob's thigh in the sinew of
the hip."*

As most of you would know, Jacob's name means usurper
or deceiver. From early in his life, aided and abetted by his
mother, he looked for a plan B to get ahead in life. Yet, in
spite his efforts to do his own thing, God blessed him. In
this part of his story, Jacob is on his way to meet his
brother. The last time they had chatted, Esau had promised
to kill Jacob, so naturally he was a bit nervous. So, like the
man of faith and valor he was, he sent his wives, children,
and gifts (bribes?) ahead of him, assuming that this might
soften Esau and save his own neck. Well, the revealing
word in the passage just read was that Jacob was
alone…without wife or kids, or servants to support him, he
was vulnerable to the Lord, who confronts him. It is true
that Jacob prevailed…but from my view that as he wrestled
with the Lord, God at any time could have killed him if that
were the plan, but his touching his hip (and permanently
dislocating it) he made the point…you belong to God
Jacob, and your destiny is you not what were, but who you
really are, the Prince of God, Israel. Was the Prince there
all along? I think so.

- Esther is a unique bible character. Brought to the
  Kingdom (Babylon, not Israel, but effecting Israel
  and salvation history) "for such a time as this"
  (Esther 4:14) the main characteristic we see in her is
  courage and unselfishness. She was just a little
  Jewish girl, with a cousin that acted as a father,

Mordecai. The story is dramatic, and yet simple, showing how one person with courage could turn things around when submitted to God. So, what does this have to do with identity? If Esther, and Mordecai, perhaps a few others including the King, did not see her as a Queen, in spite her background, all could have been lost. Our very salvation was wrapped up in her courageous act, though certainly the Lord would have found another person or another way if her mission had failed or she fai8led to rise to the occasion.

- One of my favorite characters in the Old Testament is Gideon. Gideon and his 300. But long before his 300 and the great victory over the Midianites, Gideon had no idea who he was, as evidence by the conversation with the Lord or his angel in Judges 6: 11-17

"Then the angel of the LORD came and sat under the oak that was in Ophrah, which belonged to Joash the Abiezrite as his son Gideon was beating out wheat in the wine press in order to save it *from the Midianites. The angel of the LORD appeared to him and said to him, "The LORD is with you, O valiant warrior." Then Gideon said to him, "O my lord, if the LORD is with us, why then has all this happened to us? And where are all His miracles which our fathers told us about, saying, 'Did not the LORD bring us up from Egypt?' But now the LORD has abandoned us and given us into the hand of Midian." The LORD looked at him and said, "Go in this your strength and deliver Israel from the hand of Midian. Have I not sent you?" He said to Him, "O Lord, how shall I deliver Israel? Behold, my family is*

the least in Manasseh, and I am the youngest in my father's house." But the LORD *said to him, "Surely I will be with you, and you shall defeat Midian as one man." So Gideon said to Him, "If now I have found favor in Your sight, then show me a sign that it is You who speak with me. Please do not depart from here, until I come* back *to You, and bring out my offering and lay it before You." And He said, "I will remain until you return."*

Gideon could not relate to the Lord's statement that he was a mighty man of valor...but of course, the Lord knows us better than we know ourselves. Often buried in us, even in the hurts, wounds and failures of our past can be found the very characteristics necessary for our fulfillment. Gideon had a bit of time trusting the word of the Lord, but after testing it more than once, to ensure God's favor, he went for it, and perhaps to his own surprise God was even more than he expected. A good lesson indeed. Can we, as God's chosen, holy, beloved, actually act like we are who we are? What a difference it would make.

- The little chorus went like this; Zacchaeus was a wee little man, a wee little man was he, he climbed up to the sycamore tree, for the Lord he wanted to see. And as the Savior walked that way he looked up in the tree, and he said, "Zacchaeus, you come down, for I'm going to your house today!"

As a kid growing up I often felt like Zacchaeus...not the tax collector that was despised by Jews and Gentile alike, or the sinner who Jesus brought salvation to, but the wee little man so insignificant that I would hide (perhaps like Saul, who hid in his stuff) from the Lord, thought I really wished to experience him...be noticed...have worth! Of course, in Jesus calling to Zacchaeus and inviting himself to lunch (kind of presumptuous perhaps) he found salvation, significance, and security, in his new relationship with God through Christ, and what followed was genuine repentance, including restitution. But again, what did Jesus see in the tree? A wee little man, or a son of God, deserving of salvation and a place at the table in his Kingdom. I think that later, a wonderful example for all of us.

- Peter is an obvious choice. He was a Son of Thunder, a passionate follower with occasional revelation and periodic foot in mouth disease. He was bigger than life, and when he blew it he did so with gusto...go large or go home would have been Peter's motto. His biggest boast preceded his biggest failure. In the upper room, after Jesus subtly exposes Judas as the one to betray him, Peter proclaims his willingness to die for the Lord (above all his peers no doubt). Jesus pops a hole in his ego by stating that before the rooster crows in the morning he would deny him (considered one of the worst things you could do to a friend) not once, but three times. Ouch...not very good for old Pete's self-esteem. However, along with the rebuke (Lu. 22:31-33) Jesus promised Peter that he would pray for him that his faith would not fail. What failure was Jesus praying for? Not the fact that he would betray him...that did not seem to bother Jesus as much as the possibility that Satan would sift him, could take him out, as was happening to Judas, who apparently could not see a way back after his betrayal...perhaps never embracing that Jesus was the forgiver of all sin, including his. Jesus prayed that Peter would be strong enough to return, and even prophecies it...when you return, strengthen your brothers.

Peter could strengthen his brothers, becoming the shepherd Jesus had trained him to be, but he had to overcome something in the process, like most of us. Some may need to overcome apparent strengths, like self-reliance. Others apparent weaknesses. Peter had to deal with pride, and remember all that Jesus had said. In Lu. 22:61-62, after Peters denials, "The Lord turned and looked at Peter. And Peter remembered the word of the Lord, how He had told him, "Before a rooster crows today, you will deny Me three times." [62] And he went out and wept bitterly." We don't know what Peter saw when he saw Jesus look at him. My suspicion is that he saw his compassionate love and hope for Peter, his acceptance of him though he had just denied him. There is therefore no condemnation to those in Christ did not begin with Paul's writing of the words in Romans 8. But it is interesting to note, Peter only remembered part of the word that Jesus gave him, that he would deny the Lord. That he would return must have come to him later, requiring that he choose to believe the report of the Lord regarding him, later confirmed by the fire when he three times affirmed him as a shepherd of men's souls, like the Good Shepherd himself.

- Finally, one of my favorite New Testament characters is Barnabas, the son of encouragement. Frankly, other than his quarrel with Paul, that he was later vindicated of, there seems to be nothing much you can say but good about old Barnie.

Perhaps he is one of the few unique ones…seems to have it all together from the start. When money was needed, he was the man, selling some property and giving the proceeds without strings to the apostles (which certainly got their attention). Thus, when revival broke out in Antioch, Barnabas was the likely choice to represent the apostles and ensure that they were on the right track.

He was wise as well. Seeing the grace on the people in Antioch, he put no requirements on them that would have subjected them to the harshness of the Law, such as circumcision, but got busy teaching them, calling in Paul, then called Saul to help when the work got to great. In Acts 13, it is Barnabas giving the lead…in Acts 14, it is Paul, perhaps with the stronger call and anointing, or perhaps just the stronger personality took the leadership of their international mission. When the conflict rose between Paul and Barnabas over John Mark, Barnabas cousin, mission seems to have one over grace and forgiveness, which could have been devastating for most, but Barnabas, though not heard from again in the canon of Scripture, continued to serve, as he obviously knew who he was in god, a man, sent from God, called to be an apostle…Christian tradition holds that Barnabas was martyred at Salamis, Cyprus, in AD 61.

The point of all of this is quite simple really. All of these biblical characters faced opposition, and all had divine encounters with God that allowed them to embrace what only God could see in them…. they were greater than they imagined, and more dependent on God and the community of faith than they probable knew. For all of us, knowing who we are, as we have been designed by God, is imperative to our becoming all we already are in Christ. We are new creations, holy priests, kingdom of priests in fact, bought with the price of Jesus' blood, thus while yet sinners, he died for us. Even as Jesus was full of grace and truth (thus Father and Holy Spirit are equally full of grace and truth), so are we...thus, our task is to learn to be who we are, not who we wish to be, for we will never get to where we dream. Only as we enter the dream of God which he has already given us, that we are in Christ and Christ is in us, can we be all we truly are, in him.

About the Author

Dr. Stan DeKoven is the founder and President of Vision International Ministries, with programs including:

- Vision International University
- Vision International Education Network, with Learning Centers in over 150 nations worldwide.
- Vision Publishing
- Walk in Wisdom Ministries
- International Association of Christian Counseling Profes-sionals

Further, Dr. DeKoven is the author of over 45 books and guides in practical Christian living, all of which are an outgrowth of his extensive teaching ministry both nationally and internationally.

Dr. DeKoven is a graduate of San Diego State University, (B.A. Psychology), Webster University' (M.A. Counseling), Professional School of Psychological Studies (Ph.D., Counseling Psychology) Evangelical Theological Seminary (D. Min.) and is a licensed Marriage, Family and Child Counselor. As an Ordained minister and professional caregiver and educator, he is actively establishing educational programs and counseling ministry around the world and **equipping** God's leaders to equip the saints for end-time harvest.

Sign up for his newsletter at www.drstandekoven.com

Resources

Grief Relief: On Overcoming Loss
Marriage and Family Life
Family Violence: Pattern of Destruction
Journey to Wholeness: Restoration of the Soul
Group Dynamics
Human Development
Crisis Counseling
On Belay: Introduction to Care giving
*The Healing Community: Developing the Dynamic
    Counseling Ministry*
*Patterns of Destruction: Counseling and Family
    Violence*
Assessment of Human Needs
*I Want To Be Like You Dad: Breaking Generational
    Patterns*
Parenting on Purpose
Addictions Counseling
From A Father's Heart
The Bible in Counseling
Christian Education: Principles and Practice
40 Days to the Promise
Fresh Manna
Journey to Wholeness
Journey to Old Testament
Journey to New Testament
Leadership in the Church
Visionary Leadership
Financial Integrity
New Beginnings
Prayer Power

Research Writing Made Easy
Strategic Church Administration
Supernatural Architecture
That's the Kingdom of God
Transferring the Vision
Christian Response to Crisis
Christian Response to Family Violence
Catch the Vision: How to Get a Vision for Life and Ministry
Keys to Successful Ministry from the Life of Ezra
Living in Freedom
Grace and Truth: The Twin Towers of the Father's Heart
Mentoring Mandate
Mourning into Dancing
Setting the House in Order
Seven Reasons Every Local Church Should be a Ministry Training Center
Laws of Christ
Overcomers Life
What Does God Want: A Study in Christian Life
Open Heaven

And others….

For more information on these titles and more, go to

www.booksbyvision.org

'